Power
Swap

by Steven Bu
Illustrated by Bil

OXFORD
UNIVERSITY PRESS

Pip
(Boost)

Pip is super strong! She can lift up really heavy weights, like boulders. She once lifted a skyscraper!

Jin
(Swoop)

Evan
(Flex)

Nisha
(Nimbus)

Mrs Butterworth
(cook)

It was lunchtime at Hero Academy ...

"Delicious!" said Pip with a grin. "I love power-pancakes."

"Hurry up, Pip," said Jin. "I can't wait to beat you at turbo-tennis!"

Pip smiled. She was the best in the school at turbo-tennis. "Just one more pancake," she said.

"We'll see you at the turbo-tennis court," Jin said. He put his dirty plate away and went into the sunshine with Nisha and Evan.

Pip was the only one left in the dinner hall. She gobbled down the rest of her pancake.

Pip had just finished when Mrs Butterworth appeared.

"Would you mind helping me clear away the tables, Pip?" Mrs Butterworth asked.

Pip wanted to go and join her friends, but she knew she could use her super-strength to get the job done quickly. She smiled. "Of course I'll help, Mrs Butterworth."

"Thank you," Mrs Butterworth replied. She headed off into the kitchen.

Pip stacked four tables, one on top of the other. Then she picked the whole pile up and marched across the dinner hall. "I'll be outside having fun with the others in no time," she said to herself.

Then, quite suddenly, Pip slipped on a strawberry that had fallen off Jin's plate.

She skidded along the floor and … *CRASH!* She smashed straight through a wall, landing in a pile of dust and broken bricks.

Pip stood up and looked around. She was in a room she'd never seen before.

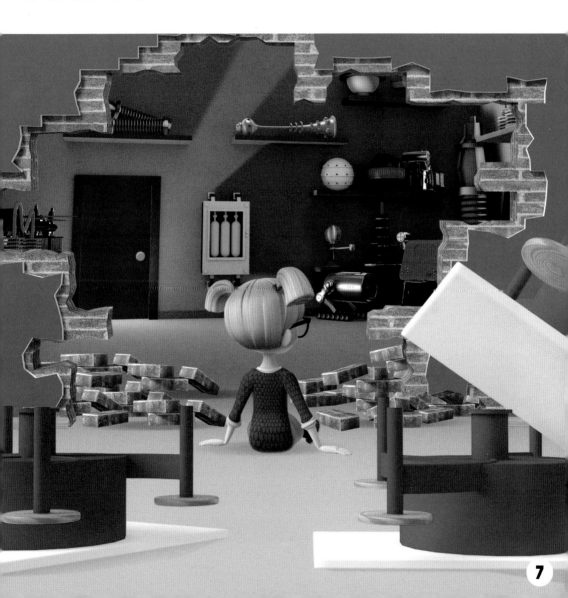

The room was filled with strange gadgets, all bleeping, flashing and ticking.

Pip gasped when she realized where she was. It was the Confiscated Gadgets Storeroom. Pupils were strictly not allowed inside.

Confiscated Gadgets Storeroom

The Confiscated Gadgets Storeroom is where the Head puts all the gadgets he has taken from baddies over the years.

Most dangerous gadget: the **Time Wobbler** – used by Mr Minute to time-travel.

Most mysterious gadget: **Gadget Number 261** – taken from Colonel Cortex in Egypt ten years ago. The Head is still trying to discover what it actually does.

Silliest gadget: the **Hover Umbrella** – with its spinning spokes, it can spin you around in the air until you're helpless with laughter.

"I should get out of here," Pip said to herself. She turned to go, but then she spotted a green, flashing ball on one of the shelves. It was covered in little buttons and was making an odd humming sound. "Ooooooooh. I wonder what this does," she said, reaching out towards it.

As she touched it, there was a sudden flash of green light and a loud *ZING!*

Pip went flying back through the hole in the wall and landed in the middle of the dinner hall with a bump. The flashing ball fell out of her hands and rolled across the floor.

"Ugh, what happened?" Pip mumbled. Her skin tingled.

Jin ran into the dinner hall. "Aaargh!" he shouted. "What's going on?" Jin started to stretch across the room like a rubber band.

Pip rubbed her eyes. Stretching wasn't Jin's superpower!

"Something's wrong!" Evan yelled, as he flew through the air and almost crashed into Jin.

"Evan, you can't fly!" Pip shouted, scrambling to her feet.

"I know," Evan said, as he whizzed past.

"I've got Evan's power, and he's got mine!" said Jin, stretching this way and that.

Pip felt a strange crackle around her hands. She looked down and saw little sparks of lightning coming out of her fingers.

"Lightning?" Pip said. "It's Nisha that can control weather ... not me!"

Nisha burst through the door with a look of shock on her face. The door smashed into the wall and giant cracks appeared.

"I'm super strong!" Nisha yelled. "What's going on?" She picked up a stack of chairs and gasped. "Pip, I've got your power!"

"Help!" Evan shouted as he bumped his head on the ceiling.

"I can't stop stretching!" Jin yelled. His arm stretched all the way down the corridor, out of the door, and then back in through a window.

"I'll stop you!" Pip said.

Pip tried to grab Jin's arm, but a storm cloud appeared above her head and started to rain on her.

Pip gasped. "It's that gadget," she said, turning towards the glowing ball. "It must have swapped all of our powers."

Just then, a blizzard of snow shot out of her fingers.

"Make some lightning, Pip," Nisha said. "ZAP THE BALL, QUICK!"

Pip watched as lots of tiny sparks raced over her hands. Having someone else's power felt so strange. What if she couldn't control it?

Pip concentrated hard and saw lightning crackling between the tips of her fingers. "Stand back, everyone," she called.

Nisha picked up a table to use as a shield. "You can do it, Pip," she said to her friend.

Pip aimed at the glowing ball. *ZAPPPPPPP!* An enormous bolt of lightning shot from her hand and hit the gadget with a massive *BOOOOM!*

The glowing ball cracked in two and a flash of green light filled the dinner hall.

"Aaargh!" Evan tumbled to the ground.

"Ooof!" Jin's arms whipped back to normal.

"Whoops!" Nisha dropped the table she'd been holding.

For a moment, nobody spoke. The four
friends looked at each other with wide eyes.

"Did that really just happen?" Jin asked.

"I think so," Pip replied, picking up the table
that Nisha had dropped. "At least I have my
own power back now."

That afternoon, Pip helped Magnus fix the hole in the wall.

Afterwards, she headed outside to meet Jin, Nisha and Evan.

"Now can we play turbo-tennis?" she asked.

Pip smiled as her friends ran off to the turbo-tennis courts.

"I'll let them win," she said to herself, with a grin. "Just this once!"